AUTOCROSS LOGBOOK

RECORD YOUR VEHICLE SETTINGS, RUN TIMES, EVENT INFORMATION, NOTES AND A COURSE SKETCH FOR TWENTY FIVE AUTOCROSS EVENTS

AUTOCROSS LOGBOOK

ISBN: 0-9768076-2-9

ISBN13: 978-0-9768076-2-9

JERA PUBLISHING

Published by Jera Publishing

an imprint of Jera Web Creations, LLC

www.jerapublishing.com

Printed in the United States of America

www.autocrosslogbook.com

AUTOCROSS
EVENTS

EVENT #1

EVENT NAME:	DATE:
LOCATION:	WEATHER:
VEHICLE MAKE:	VEHICLE MODEL:
TIRES:	FTD:
PAX RANKING:	CLASS RANK:

COURSE SKETCH:

RUN #1

	DRIVER SIDE	PASSENGER SIDE
FRONT TIRE PRESSURE		
REAR TIRE PRESSURE		
FRONT SHOCK		
REAR SHOCK		

SWAYBAR

FRONT	REAR

TIME

NOTES:

_____

_____

_____

_____

RUN #2

	DRIVER SIDE	PASSENGER SIDE
FRONT TIRE PRESSURE		
REAR TIRE PRESSURE		
FRONT SHOCK		
REAR SHOCK		

SWAYBAR

FRONT	REAR

TIME

NOTES:

_____

_____

_____

_____

AUTOCROSS LOGBOOK

RUN #3

	DRIVER SIDE	PASSENGER SIDE
FRONT TIRE PRESSURE		
REAR TIRE PRESSURE		
FRONT SHOCK		
REAR SHOCK		

SWAYBAR	
FRONT	REAR

TIME

NOTES:

_____

_____

_____

_____

RUN #4

	DRIVER SIDE	PASSENGER SIDE
FRONT TIRE PRESSURE		
REAR TIRE PRESSURE		
FRONT SHOCK		
REAR SHOCK		

SWAYBAR	
FRONT	REAR

TIME

NOTES:

_____

_____

_____

_____

RUN #5

	DRIVER SIDE	PASSENGER SIDE
FRONT TIRE PRESSURE		
REAR TIRE PRESSURE		
FRONT SHOCK		
REAR SHOCK		

SWAYBAR

FRONT	REAR

TIME

NOTES:

_____

_____

_____

_____

RUN #6

	DRIVER SIDE	PASSENGER SIDE
FRONT TIRE PRESSURE		
REAR TIRE PRESSURE		
FRONT SHOCK		
REAR SHOCK		

SWAYBAR

FRONT	REAR

TIME

NOTES:

_____

_____

_____

_____

AUTOCROSS LOGBOOK

EVENT #2

EVENT NAME:	DATE:
LOCATION:	WEATHER:
VEHICLE MAKE:	VEHICLE MODEL:
TIRES:	FTD:
PAX RANKING:	CLASS RANK:

COURSE SKETCH:

RUN #1

	DRIVER SIDE	PASSENGER SIDE
FRONT TIRE PRESSURE		
REAR TIRE PRESSURE		
FRONT SHOCK		
REAR SHOCK		

SWAYBAR

FRONT	REAR

TIME

NOTES:
_____
_____
_____
_____

RUN #2

	DRIVER SIDE	PASSENGER SIDE
FRONT TIRE PRESSURE		
REAR TIRE PRESSURE		
FRONT SHOCK		
REAR SHOCK		

SWAYBAR

FRONT	REAR

TIME

NOTES:
_____
_____
_____
_____

RUN #3

	DRIVER SIDE	PASSENGER SIDE
FRONT TIRE PRESSURE		
REAR TIRE PRESSURE		
FRONT SHOCK		
REAR SHOCK		

SWAYBAR	
FRONT	REAR

TIME

NOTES:

_____

_____

_____

_____

RUN #4

	DRIVER SIDE	PASSENGER SIDE
FRONT TIRE PRESSURE		
REAR TIRE PRESSURE		
FRONT SHOCK		
REAR SHOCK		

SWAYBAR	
FRONT	REAR

TIME

NOTES:

_____

_____

_____

_____

RUN #5

	DRIVER SIDE	PASSENGER SIDE
FRONT TIRE PRESSURE		
REAR TIRE PRESSURE		
FRONT SHOCK		
REAR SHOCK		

SWAYBAR	
FRONT	REAR

TIME

NOTES:

_____

_____

_____

_____

RUN #6

	DRIVER SIDE	PASSENGER SIDE
FRONT TIRE PRESSURE		
REAR TIRE PRESSURE		
FRONT SHOCK		
REAR SHOCK		

SWAYBAR	
FRONT	REAR

TIME

NOTES:

_____

_____

_____

EVENT #3

EVENT NAME:	DATE:
LOCATION:	WEATHER:
VEHICLE MAKE:	VEHICLE MODEL:
TIRES:	FTD:
PAX RANKING:	CLASS RANK:

COURSE SKETCH:

RUN #1

	DRIVER SIDE	PASSENGER SIDE
FRONT TIRE PRESSURE		
REAR TIRE PRESSURE		
FRONT SHOCK		
REAR SHOCK		

SWAYBAR	
FRONT	REAR

TIME

NOTES:

_____

_____

_____

_____

RUN #2

	DRIVER SIDE	PASSENGER SIDE
FRONT TIRE PRESSURE		
REAR TIRE PRESSURE		
FRONT SHOCK		
REAR SHOCK		

SWAYBAR	
FRONT	REAR

TIME

NOTES:

_____

_____

_____

RUN #3

	DRIVER SIDE	PASSENGER SIDE
FRONT TIRE PRESSURE		
REAR TIRE PRESSURE		
FRONT SHOCK		
REAR SHOCK		

SWAYBAR	
FRONT	REAR

TIME

NOTES:

_____

_____

_____

_____

RUN #4

	DRIVER SIDE	PASSENGER SIDE
FRONT TIRE PRESSURE		
REAR TIRE PRESSURE		
FRONT SHOCK		
REAR SHOCK		

SWAYBAR	
FRONT	REAR

TIME

NOTES:

_____

_____

_____

_____

RUN #5

	DRIVER SIDE	PASSENGER SIDE
FRONT TIRE PRESSURE		
REAR TIRE PRESSURE		
FRONT SHOCK		
REAR SHOCK		

SWAYBAR

FRONT	REAR

TIME

NOTES:

_____

_____

_____

_____

RUN #6

	DRIVER SIDE	PASSENGER SIDE
FRONT TIRE PRESSURE		
REAR TIRE PRESSURE		
FRONT SHOCK		
REAR SHOCK		

SWAYBAR

FRONT	REAR

TIME

NOTES:

_____

_____

_____

_____

EVENT #4

EVENT NAME:	DATE:
LOCATION:	WEATHER:
VEHICLE MAKE:	VEHICLE MODEL:
TIRES:	FTD:
PAX RANKING:	CLASS RANK:

COURSE SKETCH:

RUN #1

	DRIVER SIDE	PASSENGER SIDE
FRONT TIRE PRESSURE		
REAR TIRE PRESSURE		
FRONT SHOCK		
REAR SHOCK		

SWAYBAR	
FRONT	REAR

TIME

NOTES:

_____

_____

_____

_____

RUN #2

	DRIVER SIDE	PASSENGER SIDE
FRONT TIRE PRESSURE		
REAR TIRE PRESSURE		
FRONT SHOCK		
REAR SHOCK		

SWAYBAR	
FRONT	REAR

TIME

NOTES:

_____

_____

_____

_____

RUN #3

	DRIVER SIDE	PASSENGER SIDE
FRONT TIRE PRESSURE		
REAR TIRE PRESSURE		
FRONT SHOCK		
REAR SHOCK		

SWAYBAR	
FRONT	REAR

TIME

NOTES:

_____

_____

_____

_____

RUN #4

	DRIVER SIDE	PASSENGER SIDE
FRONT TIRE PRESSURE		
REAR TIRE PRESSURE		
FRONT SHOCK		
REAR SHOCK		

SWAYBAR	
FRONT	REAR

TIME

NOTES:

_____

_____

_____

_____

RUN #5

	DRIVER SIDE	PASSENGER SIDE
FRONT TIRE PRESSURE		
REAR TIRE PRESSURE		
FRONT SHOCK		
REAR SHOCK		

SWAYBAR

FRONT	REAR

TIME

NOTES:

_____

_____

_____

_____

RUN #6

	DRIVER SIDE	PASSENGER SIDE
FRONT TIRE PRESSURE		
REAR TIRE PRESSURE		
FRONT SHOCK		
REAR SHOCK		

SWAYBAR

FRONT	REAR

TIME

NOTES:

_____

_____

_____

_____

EVENT #5

EVENT NAME:	DATE:
LOCATION:	WEATHER:
VEHICLE MAKE:	VEHICLE MODEL:
TIRES:	FTD:
PAX RANKING:	CLASS RANK:

COURSE SKETCH:

RUN #1

	DRIVER SIDE	PASSENGER SIDE
FRONT TIRE PRESSURE		
REAR TIRE PRESSURE		
FRONT SHOCK		
REAR SHOCK		

SWAYBAR	
FRONT	REAR

TIME

NOTES:

_____

_____

_____

_____

RUN #2

	DRIVER SIDE	PASSENGER SIDE
FRONT TIRE PRESSURE		
REAR TIRE PRESSURE		
FRONT SHOCK		
REAR SHOCK		

SWAYBAR	
FRONT	REAR

TIME

NOTES:

_____

_____

_____

_____

RUN #3

	DRIVER SIDE	PASSENGER SIDE
FRONT TIRE PRESSURE		
REAR TIRE PRESSURE		
FRONT SHOCK		
REAR SHOCK		

SWAYBAR	
FRONT	REAR

TIME

NOTES:

_____

_____

_____

_____

RUN #4

	DRIVER SIDE	PASSENGER SIDE
FRONT TIRE PRESSURE		
REAR TIRE PRESSURE		
FRONT SHOCK		
REAR SHOCK		

SWAYBAR	
FRONT	REAR

TIME

NOTES:

_____

_____

_____

_____

RUN #5

	DRIVER SIDE	PASSENGER SIDE
FRONT TIRE PRESSURE		
REAR TIRE PRESSURE		
FRONT SHOCK		
REAR SHOCK		

SWAYBAR

FRONT	REAR

TIME

NOTES:

_____

_____

_____

_____

RUN #6

	DRIVER SIDE	PASSENGER SIDE
FRONT TIRE PRESSURE		
REAR TIRE PRESSURE		
FRONT SHOCK		
REAR SHOCK		

SWAYBAR

FRONT	REAR

TIME

NOTES:

_____

_____

_____

_____

EVENT #6

EVENT NAME: | DATE:

LOCATION: | WEATHER:

VEHICLE MAKE: | VEHICLE MODEL:

TIRES: | FTD:

PAX RANKING: | CLASS RANK:

COURSE SKETCH:

RUN #1

	DRIVER SIDE	PASSENGER SIDE
FRONT TIRE PRESSURE		
REAR TIRE PRESSURE		
FRONT SHOCK		
REAR SHOCK		

SWAYBAR	
FRONT	REAR

TIME

NOTES:

_____

_____

_____

_____

RUN #2

	DRIVER SIDE	PASSENGER SIDE
FRONT TIRE PRESSURE		
REAR TIRE PRESSURE		
FRONT SHOCK		
REAR SHOCK		

SWAYBAR	
FRONT	REAR

TIME

NOTES:

_____

_____

_____

_____

RUN #3

	DRIVER SIDE	PASSENGER SIDE
FRONT TIRE PRESSURE		
REAR TIRE PRESSURE		
FRONT SHOCK		
REAR SHOCK		

SWAYBAR

FRONT	REAR

TIME

NOTES:

_____

_____

_____

_____

RUN #4

	DRIVER SIDE	PASSENGER SIDE
FRONT TIRE PRESSURE		
REAR TIRE PRESSURE		
FRONT SHOCK		
REAR SHOCK		

SWAYBAR

FRONT	REAR

TIME

NOTES:

_____

_____

_____

_____

RUN #5

	DRIVER SIDE	PASSENGER SIDE
FRONT TIRE PRESSURE		
REAR TIRE PRESSURE		
FRONT SHOCK		
REAR SHOCK		

SWAYBAR	
FRONT	REAR

TIME

NOTES:

_____

_____

_____

_____

RUN #6

	DRIVER SIDE	PASSENGER SIDE
FRONT TIRE PRESSURE		
REAR TIRE PRESSURE		
FRONT SHOCK		
REAR SHOCK		

SWAYBAR	
FRONT	REAR

TIME

NOTES:

_____

_____

_____

EVENT #7

EVENT NAME:	DATE:
LOCATION:	WEATHER:
VEHICLE MAKE:	VEHICLE MODEL:
TIRES:	FTD:
PAX RANKING:	CLASS RANK:

COURSE SKETCH:

RUN #1

	DRIVER SIDE	PASSENGER SIDE
FRONT TIRE PRESSURE		
REAR TIRE PRESSURE		
FRONT SHOCK		
REAR SHOCK		

SWAYBAR

FRONT	REAR

TIME

NOTES:

_____

_____

_____

_____

RUN #2

	DRIVER SIDE	PASSENGER SIDE
FRONT TIRE PRESSURE		
REAR TIRE PRESSURE		
FRONT SHOCK		
REAR SHOCK		

SWAYBAR

FRONT	REAR

TIME

NOTES:

_____

_____

_____

_____

RUN #3

	DRIVER SIDE	PASSENGER SIDE
FRONT TIRE PRESSURE		
REAR TIRE PRESSURE		
FRONT SHOCK		
REAR SHOCK		

SWAYBAR

FRONT	REAR

TIME

NOTES:

_____

_____

_____

RUN #4

	DRIVER SIDE	PASSENGER SIDE
FRONT TIRE PRESSURE		
REAR TIRE PRESSURE		
FRONT SHOCK		
REAR SHOCK		

SWAYBAR

FRONT	REAR

TIME

NOTES:

_____

_____

_____

RUN #5

	DRIVER SIDE	PASSENGER SIDE
FRONT TIRE PRESSURE		
REAR TIRE PRESSURE		
FRONT SHOCK		
REAR SHOCK		

SWAYBAR

FRONT	REAR

TIME

NOTES:

_____

_____

_____

_____

RUN #6

	DRIVER SIDE	PASSENGER SIDE
FRONT TIRE PRESSURE		
REAR TIRE PRESSURE		
FRONT SHOCK		
REAR SHOCK		

SWAYBAR

FRONT	REAR

TIME

NOTES:

_____

_____

_____

EVENT #8

EVENT NAME:	DATE:
LOCATION:	WEATHER:
VEHICLE MAKE:	VEHICLE MODEL:
TIRES:	FTD:
PAX RANKING:	CLASS RANK:

COURSE SKETCH:

RUN #1

	DRIVER SIDE	PASSENGER SIDE
FRONT TIRE PRESSURE		
REAR TIRE PRESSURE		
FRONT SHOCK		
REAR SHOCK		

SWAYBAR

FRONT	REAR

TIME

NOTES:

_____

_____

_____

_____

RUN #2

	DRIVER SIDE	PASSENGER SIDE
FRONT TIRE PRESSURE		
REAR TIRE PRESSURE		
FRONT SHOCK		
REAR SHOCK		

SWAYBAR

FRONT	REAR

TIME

NOTES:

_____

_____

_____

_____

RUN #3

	DRIVER SIDE	PASSENGER SIDE
FRONT TIRE PRESSURE		
REAR TIRE PRESSURE		
FRONT SHOCK		
REAR SHOCK		

SWAYBAR	
FRONT	REAR

TIME

NOTES:

_____

_____

_____

_____

RUN #4

	DRIVER SIDE	PASSENGER SIDE
FRONT TIRE PRESSURE		
REAR TIRE PRESSURE		
FRONT SHOCK		
REAR SHOCK		

SWAYBAR	
FRONT	REAR

TIME

NOTES:

_____

_____

_____

_____

RUN #5

	DRIVER SIDE	PASSENGER SIDE
FRONT TIRE PRESSURE		
REAR TIRE PRESSURE		
FRONT SHOCK		
REAR SHOCK		

SWAYBAR

FRONT	REAR

TIME

NOTES:

_____

_____

_____

_____

RUN #6

	DRIVER SIDE	PASSENGER SIDE
FRONT TIRE PRESSURE		
REAR TIRE PRESSURE		
FRONT SHOCK		
REAR SHOCK		

SWAYBAR

FRONT	REAR

TIME

NOTES:

_____

_____

_____

_____

EVENT #9

EVENT NAME:	DATE:
LOCATION:	WEATHER:
VEHICLE MAKE:	VEHICLE MODEL:
TIRES:	FTD:
PAX RANKING:	CLASS RANK:

COURSE SKETCH:

RUN #1

	DRIVER SIDE	PASSENGER SIDE
FRONT TIRE PRESSURE		
REAR TIRE PRESSURE		
FRONT SHOCK		
REAR SHOCK		

SWAYBAR

FRONT	REAR

TIME

NOTES:

_____

_____

_____

_____

RUN #2

	DRIVER SIDE	PASSENGER SIDE
FRONT TIRE PRESSURE		
REAR TIRE PRESSURE		
FRONT SHOCK		
REAR SHOCK		

SWAYBAR

FRONT	REAR

TIME

NOTES:

_____

_____

_____

_____

RUN #3

	DRIVER SIDE	PASSENGER SIDE
FRONT TIRE PRESSURE		
REAR TIRE PRESSURE		
FRONT SHOCK		
REAR SHOCK		

SWAYBAR	
FRONT	REAR

TIME

NOTES:

_____

_____

_____

_____

RUN #4

	DRIVER SIDE	PASSENGER SIDE
FRONT TIRE PRESSURE		
REAR TIRE PRESSURE		
FRONT SHOCK		
REAR SHOCK		

SWAYBAR	
FRONT	REAR

TIME

NOTES:

_____

_____

_____

_____

RUN #5

	DRIVER SIDE	PASSENGER SIDE
FRONT TIRE PRESSURE		
REAR TIRE PRESSURE		
FRONT SHOCK		
REAR SHOCK		

SWAYBAR

FRONT	REAR

TIME

NOTES:

_____

_____

_____

_____

RUN #6

	DRIVER SIDE	PASSENGER SIDE
FRONT TIRE PRESSURE		
REAR TIRE PRESSURE		
FRONT SHOCK		
REAR SHOCK		

SWAYBAR

FRONT	REAR

TIME

NOTES:

_____

_____

_____

_____

EVENT #10

EVENT NAME:

DATE:

LOCATION:

WEATHER:

VEHICLE MAKE:

VEHICLE MODEL:

TIRES:

FTD:

PAX RANKING:

CLASS RANK:

COURSE SKETCH:

RUN #1

	DRIVER SIDE	PASSENGER SIDE
FRONT TIRE PRESSURE		
REAR TIRE PRESSURE		
FRONT SHOCK		
REAR SHOCK		

SWAYBAR	
FRONT	REAR

TIME

NOTES:

_____

_____

_____

_____

RUN #2

	DRIVER SIDE	PASSENGER SIDE
FRONT TIRE PRESSURE		
REAR TIRE PRESSURE		
FRONT SHOCK		
REAR SHOCK		

SWAYBAR	
FRONT	REAR

TIME

NOTES:

_____

_____

_____

_____

RUN #3

	DRIVER SIDE	PASSENGER SIDE
FRONT TIRE PRESSURE		
REAR TIRE PRESSURE		
FRONT SHOCK		
REAR SHOCK		

SWAYBAR	
FRONT	REAR

TIME

NOTES:

_____

_____

_____

_____

RUN #4

	DRIVER SIDE	PASSENGER SIDE
FRONT TIRE PRESSURE		
REAR TIRE PRESSURE		
FRONT SHOCK		
REAR SHOCK		

SWAYBAR	
FRONT	REAR

TIME

NOTES:

_____

_____

_____

_____

RUN #5

	DRIVER SIDE	PASSENGER SIDE
FRONT TIRE PRESSURE		
REAR TIRE PRESSURE		
FRONT SHOCK		
REAR SHOCK		

SWAYBAR

FRONT	REAR

TIME

NOTES:

_____

_____

_____

_____

RUN #6

	DRIVER SIDE	PASSENGER SIDE
FRONT TIRE PRESSURE		
REAR TIRE PRESSURE		
FRONT SHOCK		
REAR SHOCK		

SWAYBAR

FRONT	REAR

TIME

NOTES:

_____

_____

_____

_____

EVENT #11

EVENT NAME:	DATE:
LOCATION:	WEATHER:
VEHICLE MAKE:	VEHICLE MODEL:
TIRES:	FTD:
PAX RANKING:	CLASS RANK:

COURSE SKETCH:

RUN #1

	DRIVER SIDE	PASSENGER SIDE
FRONT TIRE PRESSURE		
REAR TIRE PRESSURE		
FRONT SHOCK		
REAR SHOCK		

SWAYBAR

FRONT	REAR

TIME

NOTES:

_____

_____

_____

_____

RUN #2

	DRIVER SIDE	PASSENGER SIDE
FRONT TIRE PRESSURE		
REAR TIRE PRESSURE		
FRONT SHOCK		
REAR SHOCK		

SWAYBAR

FRONT	REAR

TIME

NOTES:

_____

_____

_____

_____

RUN #3

	DRIVER SIDE	PASSENGER SIDE
FRONT TIRE PRESSURE		
REAR TIRE PRESSURE		
FRONT SHOCK		
REAR SHOCK		

SWAYBAR

FRONT	REAR

TIME

NOTES:

_____

_____

_____

_____

RUN #4

	DRIVER SIDE	PASSENGER SIDE
FRONT TIRE PRESSURE		
REAR TIRE PRESSURE		
FRONT SHOCK		
REAR SHOCK		

SWAYBAR

FRONT	REAR

TIME

NOTES:

_____

_____

_____

_____

RUN #5

	DRIVER SIDE	PASSENGER SIDE
FRONT TIRE PRESSURE		
REAR TIRE PRESSURE		
FRONT SHOCK		
REAR SHOCK		

SWAYBAR

FRONT	REAR

TIME

NOTES:

_____

_____

_____

_____

RUN #6

	DRIVER SIDE	PASSENGER SIDE
FRONT TIRE PRESSURE		
REAR TIRE PRESSURE		
FRONT SHOCK		
REAR SHOCK		

SWAYBAR

FRONT	REAR

TIME

NOTES:

_____

_____

_____

_____

EVENT #12

EVENT NAME:	DATE:
LOCATION:	WEATHER:
VEHICLE MAKE:	VEHICLE MODEL:
TIRES:	FTD:
PAX RANKING:	CLASS RANK:

COURSE SKETCH:

RUN #1

	DRIVER SIDE	PASSENGER SIDE
FRONT TIRE PRESSURE		
REAR TIRE PRESSURE		
FRONT SHOCK		
REAR SHOCK		

SWAYBAR	
FRONT	REAR

TIME

NOTES:

_____

_____

_____

_____

RUN #2

	DRIVER SIDE	PASSENGER SIDE
FRONT TIRE PRESSURE		
REAR TIRE PRESSURE		
FRONT SHOCK		
REAR SHOCK		

SWAYBAR	
FRONT	REAR

TIME

NOTES:

_____

_____

_____

_____

RUN #3

	DRIVER SIDE	PASSENGER SIDE
FRONT TIRE PRESSURE		
REAR TIRE PRESSURE		
FRONT SHOCK		
REAR SHOCK		

SWAYBAR	
FRONT	REAR

TIME

NOTES:

_____

_____

_____

_____

RUN #4

	DRIVER SIDE	PASSENGER SIDE
FRONT TIRE PRESSURE		
REAR TIRE PRESSURE		
FRONT SHOCK		
REAR SHOCK		

SWAYBAR	
FRONT	REAR

TIME

NOTES:

_____

_____

_____

_____

RUN #5

	DRIVER SIDE	PASSENGER SIDE
FRONT TIRE PRESSURE		
REAR TIRE PRESSURE		
FRONT SHOCK		
REAR SHOCK		

SWAYBAR	
FRONT	REAR

TIME

NOTES:

_____

_____

_____

_____

RUN #6

	DRIVER SIDE	PASSENGER SIDE
FRONT TIRE PRESSURE		
REAR TIRE PRESSURE		
FRONT SHOCK		
REAR SHOCK		

SWAYBAR	
FRONT	REAR

TIME

NOTES:

_____

_____

_____

_____

EVENT #13

EVENT NAME:	DATE:
LOCATION:	WEATHER:
VEHICLE MAKE:	VEHICLE MODEL:
TIRES:	FTD:
PAX RANKING:	CLASS RANK:

COURSE SKETCH:

RUN #1

	DRIVER SIDE	PASSENGER SIDE
FRONT TIRE PRESSURE		
REAR TIRE PRESSURE		
FRONT SHOCK		
REAR SHOCK		

SWAYBAR

FRONT	REAR

TIME

NOTES:

_____

_____

_____

_____

RUN #2

	DRIVER SIDE	PASSENGER SIDE
FRONT TIRE PRESSURE		
REAR TIRE PRESSURE		
FRONT SHOCK		
REAR SHOCK		

SWAYBAR

FRONT	REAR

TIME

NOTES:

_____

_____

_____

_____

RUN #3

	DRIVER SIDE	PASSENGER SIDE
FRONT TIRE PRESSURE		
REAR TIRE PRESSURE		
FRONT SHOCK		
REAR SHOCK		

SWAYBAR	
FRONT	REAR

TIME

NOTES:

_____

_____

_____

_____

RUN #4

	DRIVER SIDE	PASSENGER SIDE
FRONT TIRE PRESSURE		
REAR TIRE PRESSURE		
FRONT SHOCK		
REAR SHOCK		

SWAYBAR	
FRONT	REAR

TIME

NOTES:

_____

_____

_____

_____

RUN #5

	DRIVER SIDE	PASSENGER SIDE
FRONT TIRE PRESSURE		
REAR TIRE PRESSURE		
FRONT SHOCK		
REAR SHOCK		

SWAYBAR

FRONT	REAR

TIME

NOTES:

_____

_____

_____

_____

RUN #6

	DRIVER SIDE	PASSENGER SIDE
FRONT TIRE PRESSURE		
REAR TIRE PRESSURE		
FRONT SHOCK		
REAR SHOCK		

SWAYBAR

FRONT	REAR

TIME

NOTES:

_____

_____

_____

_____

EVENT #14

EVENT NAME:	DATE:
LOCATION:	WEATHER:
VEHICLE MAKE:	VEHICLE MODEL:
TIRES:	FTD:
PAX RANKING:	CLASS RANK:

COURSE SKETCH:

RUN #1

	DRIVER SIDE	PASSENGER SIDE
FRONT TIRE PRESSURE		
REAR TIRE PRESSURE		
FRONT SHOCK		
REAR SHOCK		

SWAYBAR

FRONT	REAR

TIME

NOTES:

_____

_____

_____

_____

RUN #2

	DRIVER SIDE	PASSENGER SIDE
FRONT TIRE PRESSURE		
REAR TIRE PRESSURE		
FRONT SHOCK		
REAR SHOCK		

SWAYBAR

FRONT	REAR

TIME

NOTES:

_____

_____

_____

_____

RUN #3

	DRIVER SIDE	PASSENGER SIDE
FRONT TIRE PRESSURE		
REAR TIRE PRESSURE		
FRONT SHOCK		
REAR SHOCK		

SWAYBAR

FRONT	REAR

TIME

NOTES:

_____

_____

_____

_____

RUN #4

	DRIVER SIDE	PASSENGER SIDE
FRONT TIRE PRESSURE		
REAR TIRE PRESSURE		
FRONT SHOCK		
REAR SHOCK		

SWAYBAR

FRONT	REAR

TIME

NOTES:

_____

_____

_____

_____

RUN #5

	DRIVER SIDE	PASSENGER SIDE
FRONT TIRE PRESSURE		
REAR TIRE PRESSURE		
FRONT SHOCK		
REAR SHOCK		

SWAYBAR

FRONT	REAR

TIME

NOTES:

_____

_____

_____

_____

RUN #6

	DRIVER SIDE	PASSENGER SIDE
FRONT TIRE PRESSURE		
REAR TIRE PRESSURE		
FRONT SHOCK		
REAR SHOCK		

SWAYBAR

FRONT	REAR

TIME

NOTES:

_____

_____

_____

_____

EVENT #15

EVENT NAME:	DATE:
LOCATION:	WEATHER:
VEHICLE MAKE:	VEHICLE MODEL:
TIRES:	FTD:
PAX RANKING:	CLASS RANK:

COURSE SKETCH:

RUN #1

	DRIVER SIDE	PASSENGER SIDE
FRONT TIRE PRESSURE		
REAR TIRE PRESSURE		
FRONT SHOCK		
REAR SHOCK		

SWAYBAR

FRONT	REAR

TIME

NOTES:

_____

_____

_____

_____

RUN #2

	DRIVER SIDE	PASSENGER SIDE
FRONT TIRE PRESSURE		
REAR TIRE PRESSURE		
FRONT SHOCK		
REAR SHOCK		

SWAYBAR

FRONT	REAR

TIME

NOTES:

_____

_____

_____

_____

RUN #3

	DRIVER SIDE	PASSENGER SIDE
FRONT TIRE PRESSURE		
REAR TIRE PRESSURE		
FRONT SHOCK		
REAR SHOCK		

SWAYBAR	
FRONT	REAR

TIME

NOTES:

_____

_____

_____

_____

RUN #4

	DRIVER SIDE	PASSENGER SIDE
FRONT TIRE PRESSURE		
REAR TIRE PRESSURE		
FRONT SHOCK		
REAR SHOCK		

SWAYBAR	
FRONT	REAR

TIME

NOTES:

_____

_____

_____

_____

RUN #5

	DRIVER SIDE	PASSENGER SIDE
FRONT TIRE PRESSURE		
REAR TIRE PRESSURE		
FRONT SHOCK		
REAR SHOCK		

SWAYBAR	
FRONT	REAR

TIME

NOTES:

_____

_____

_____

_____

RUN #6

	DRIVER SIDE	PASSENGER SIDE
FRONT TIRE PRESSURE		
REAR TIRE PRESSURE		
FRONT SHOCK		
REAR SHOCK		

SWAYBAR	
FRONT	REAR

TIME

NOTES:

_____

_____

_____

_____

EVENT #16

EVENT NAME:	DATE:
LOCATION:	WEATHER:
VEHICLE MAKE:	VEHICLE MODEL:
TIRES:	FTD:
PAX RANKING:	CLASS RANK:

COURSE SKETCH:

RUN #1

	DRIVER SIDE	PASSENGER SIDE
FRONT TIRE PRESSURE		
REAR TIRE PRESSURE		
FRONT SHOCK		
REAR SHOCK		

SWAYBAR	
FRONT	REAR

TIME

NOTES:

_____

_____

_____

_____

RUN #2

	DRIVER SIDE	PASSENGER SIDE
FRONT TIRE PRESSURE		
REAR TIRE PRESSURE		
FRONT SHOCK		
REAR SHOCK		

SWAYBAR	
FRONT	REAR

TIME

NOTES:

_____

_____

_____

_____

RUN #3

	DRIVER SIDE	PASSENGER SIDE
FRONT TIRE PRESSURE		
REAR TIRE PRESSURE		
FRONT SHOCK		
REAR SHOCK		

SWAYBAR	
FRONT	REAR

TIME

NOTES:

_____

_____

_____

_____

RUN #4

	DRIVER SIDE	PASSENGER SIDE
FRONT TIRE PRESSURE		
REAR TIRE PRESSURE		
FRONT SHOCK		
REAR SHOCK		

SWAYBAR	
FRONT	REAR

TIME

NOTES:

_____

_____

_____

_____

RUN #5

	DRIVER SIDE	PASSENGER SIDE
FRONT TIRE PRESSURE		
REAR TIRE PRESSURE		
FRONT SHOCK		
REAR SHOCK		

SWAYBAR

FRONT	REAR

TIME

NOTES:

_____

_____

_____

_____

RUN #6

	DRIVER SIDE	PASSENGER SIDE
FRONT TIRE PRESSURE		
REAR TIRE PRESSURE		
FRONT SHOCK		
REAR SHOCK		

SWAYBAR

FRONT	REAR

TIME

NOTES:

_____

_____

_____

_____

EVENT #17

EVENT NAME: DATE:

LOCATION: WEATHER:

VEHICLE MAKE: VEHICLE MODEL:

TIRES: FTD:

PAX RANKING: CLASS RANK:

COURSE SKETCH:

RUN #1

	DRIVER SIDE	PASSENGER SIDE
FRONT TIRE PRESSURE		
REAR TIRE PRESSURE		
FRONT SHOCK		
REAR SHOCK		

SWAYBAR

FRONT	REAR

TIME

NOTES:

_____

_____

_____

_____

RUN #2

	DRIVER SIDE	PASSENGER SIDE
FRONT TIRE PRESSURE		
REAR TIRE PRESSURE		
FRONT SHOCK		
REAR SHOCK		

SWAYBAR

FRONT	REAR

TIME

NOTES:

_____

_____

_____

_____

RUN #3

	DRIVER SIDE	PASSENGER SIDE
FRONT TIRE PRESSURE		
REAR TIRE PRESSURE		
FRONT SHOCK		
REAR SHOCK		

SWAYBAR	
FRONT	REAR

TIME

NOTES:

_____

_____

_____

_____

RUN #4

	DRIVER SIDE	PASSENGER SIDE
FRONT TIRE PRESSURE		
REAR TIRE PRESSURE		
FRONT SHOCK		
REAR SHOCK		

SWAYBAR	
FRONT	REAR

TIME

NOTES:

_____

_____

_____

_____

RUN #5

	DRIVER SIDE	PASSENGER SIDE
FRONT TIRE PRESSURE		
REAR TIRE PRESSURE		
FRONT SHOCK		
REAR SHOCK		

SWAYBAR

FRONT	REAR

TIME

NOTES:

_____

_____

_____

_____

RUN #6

	DRIVER SIDE	PASSENGER SIDE
FRONT TIRE PRESSURE		
REAR TIRE PRESSURE		
FRONT SHOCK		
REAR SHOCK		

SWAYBAR

FRONT	REAR

TIME

NOTES:

_____

_____

_____

_____

EVENT #18

EVENT NAME: DATE:

LOCATION: WEATHER:

VEHICLE MAKE: VEHICLE MODEL:

TIRES: FTD:

PAX RANKING: CLASS RANK:

COURSE SKETCH:

RUN #1

	DRIVER SIDE	PASSENGER SIDE
FRONT TIRE PRESSURE		
REAR TIRE PRESSURE		
FRONT SHOCK		
REAR SHOCK		

SWAYBAR

FRONT	REAR

TIME

NOTES:

_____

_____

_____

_____

RUN #2

	DRIVER SIDE	PASSENGER SIDE
FRONT TIRE PRESSURE		
REAR TIRE PRESSURE		
FRONT SHOCK		
REAR SHOCK		

SWAYBAR

FRONT	REAR

TIME

NOTES:

_____

_____

_____

_____

RUN #3

	DRIVER SIDE	PASSENGER SIDE
FRONT TIRE PRESSURE		
REAR TIRE PRESSURE		
FRONT SHOCK		
REAR SHOCK		

SWAYBAR	
FRONT	REAR

TIME

NOTES:

_____

_____

_____

_____

RUN #4

	DRIVER SIDE	PASSENGER SIDE
FRONT TIRE PRESSURE		
REAR TIRE PRESSURE		
FRONT SHOCK		
REAR SHOCK		

SWAYBAR	
FRONT	REAR

TIME

NOTES:

_____

_____

_____

_____

RUN #5

	DRIVER SIDE	PASSENGER SIDE
FRONT TIRE PRESSURE		
REAR TIRE PRESSURE		
FRONT SHOCK		
REAR SHOCK		

SWAYBAR

FRONT	REAR

TIME

NOTES:

_____

_____

_____

_____

RUN #6

	DRIVER SIDE	PASSENGER SIDE
FRONT TIRE PRESSURE		
REAR TIRE PRESSURE		
FRONT SHOCK		
REAR SHOCK		

SWAYBAR

FRONT	REAR

TIME

NOTES:

_____

_____

_____

_____

EVENT #19

EVENT NAME:	DATE:
LOCATION:	WEATHER:
VEHICLE MAKE:	VEHICLE MODEL:
TIRES:	FTD:
PAX RANKING:	CLASS RANK:

COURSE SKETCH:

RUN #1

	DRIVER SIDE	PASSENGER SIDE
FRONT TIRE PRESSURE		
REAR TIRE PRESSURE		
FRONT SHOCK		
REAR SHOCK		

SWAYBAR

FRONT	REAR

TIME

NOTES:

_____

_____

_____

_____

RUN #2

	DRIVER SIDE	PASSENGER SIDE
FRONT TIRE PRESSURE		
REAR TIRE PRESSURE		
FRONT SHOCK		
REAR SHOCK		

SWAYBAR

FRONT	REAR

TIME

NOTES:

_____

_____

_____

_____

RUN #3

	DRIVER SIDE	PASSENGER SIDE
FRONT TIRE PRESSURE		
REAR TIRE PRESSURE		
FRONT SHOCK		
REAR SHOCK		

SWAYBAR

FRONT	REAR

TIME

NOTES:

_____

_____

_____

_____

RUN #4

	DRIVER SIDE	PASSENGER SIDE
FRONT TIRE PRESSURE		
REAR TIRE PRESSURE		
FRONT SHOCK		
REAR SHOCK		

SWAYBAR

FRONT	REAR

TIME

NOTES:

_____

_____

_____

_____

RUN #5

	DRIVER SIDE	PASSENGER SIDE
FRONT TIRE PRESSURE		
REAR TIRE PRESSURE		
FRONT SHOCK		
REAR SHOCK		

SWAYBAR

FRONT	REAR

TIME

NOTES:

_____

_____

_____

_____

RUN #6

	DRIVER SIDE	PASSENGER SIDE
FRONT TIRE PRESSURE		
REAR TIRE PRESSURE		
FRONT SHOCK		
REAR SHOCK		

SWAYBAR

FRONT	REAR

TIME

NOTES:

_____

_____

_____

_____

EVENT #20

EVENT NAME:	DATE:
LOCATION:	WEATHER:
VEHICLE MAKE:	VEHICLE MODEL:
TIRES:	FTD:
PAX RANKING:	CLASS RANK:

COURSE SKETCH:

RUN #1

	DRIVER SIDE	PASSENGER SIDE
FRONT TIRE PRESSURE		
REAR TIRE PRESSURE		
FRONT SHOCK		
REAR SHOCK		

SWAYBAR

FRONT	REAR

TIME

NOTES:
_____
_____
_____
_____

RUN #2

	DRIVER SIDE	PASSENGER SIDE
FRONT TIRE PRESSURE		
REAR TIRE PRESSURE		
FRONT SHOCK		
REAR SHOCK		

SWAYBAR

FRONT	REAR

TIME

NOTES:
_____
_____
_____
_____

RUN #3

	DRIVER SIDE	PASSENGER SIDE
FRONT TIRE PRESSURE		
REAR TIRE PRESSURE		
FRONT SHOCK		
REAR SHOCK		

SWAYBAR

FRONT	REAR

TIME

NOTES:

_____

_____

_____

_____

RUN #4

	DRIVER SIDE	PASSENGER SIDE
FRONT TIRE PRESSURE		
REAR TIRE PRESSURE		
FRONT SHOCK		
REAR SHOCK		

SWAYBAR

FRONT	REAR

TIME

NOTES:

_____

_____

_____

_____

RUN #5

	DRIVER SIDE	PASSENGER SIDE
FRONT TIRE PRESSURE		
REAR TIRE PRESSURE		
FRONT SHOCK		
REAR SHOCK		

SWAYBAR

FRONT	REAR

TIME

NOTES:

_____

_____

_____

_____

RUN #6

	DRIVER SIDE	PASSENGER SIDE
FRONT TIRE PRESSURE		
REAR TIRE PRESSURE		
FRONT SHOCK		
REAR SHOCK		

SWAYBAR

FRONT	REAR

TIME

NOTES:

_____

_____

_____

_____

EVENT #21

EVENT NAME:

DATE:

LOCATION:

WEATHER:

VEHICLE MAKE:

VEHICLE MODEL:

TIRES:

FTD:

PAX RANKING:

CLASS RANK:

COURSE SKETCH:

RUN #1

	DRIVER SIDE	PASSENGER SIDE
FRONT TIRE PRESSURE		
REAR TIRE PRESSURE		
FRONT SHOCK		
REAR SHOCK		

SWAYBAR

FRONT	REAR

TIME

NOTES:

_____

_____

_____

_____

RUN #2

	DRIVER SIDE	PASSENGER SIDE
FRONT TIRE PRESSURE		
REAR TIRE PRESSURE		
FRONT SHOCK		
REAR SHOCK		

SWAYBAR

FRONT	REAR

TIME

NOTES:

_____

_____

_____

_____

RUN #3

	DRIVER SIDE	PASSENGER SIDE
FRONT TIRE PRESSURE		
REAR TIRE PRESSURE		
FRONT SHOCK		
REAR SHOCK		

SWAYBAR

FRONT	REAR

TIME

NOTES:

_____

_____

_____

_____

RUN #4

	DRIVER SIDE	PASSENGER SIDE
FRONT TIRE PRESSURE		
REAR TIRE PRESSURE		
FRONT SHOCK		
REAR SHOCK		

SWAYBAR

FRONT	REAR

TIME

NOTES:

_____

_____

_____

_____

RUN #5

	DRIVER SIDE	PASSENGER SIDE
FRONT TIRE PRESSURE		
REAR TIRE PRESSURE		
FRONT SHOCK		
REAR SHOCK		

SWAYBAR

FRONT	REAR

TIME

NOTES:
_____
_____
_____
_____

RUN #6

	DRIVER SIDE	PASSENGER SIDE
FRONT TIRE PRESSURE		
REAR TIRE PRESSURE		
FRONT SHOCK		
REAR SHOCK		

SWAYBAR

FRONT	REAR

TIME

NOTES:
_____
_____
_____
_____

EVENT #22

EVENT NAME:	DATE:
LOCATION:	WEATHER:
VEHICLE MAKE:	VEHICLE MODEL:
TIRES:	FTD:
PAX RANKING:	CLASS RANK:

COURSE SKETCH:

RUN #1

	DRIVER SIDE	PASSENGER SIDE
FRONT TIRE PRESSURE		
REAR TIRE PRESSURE		
FRONT SHOCK		
REAR SHOCK		

SWAYBAR

FRONT	REAR

TIME

NOTES:

_____

_____

_____

_____

RUN #2

	DRIVER SIDE	PASSENGER SIDE
FRONT TIRE PRESSURE		
REAR TIRE PRESSURE		
FRONT SHOCK		
REAR SHOCK		

SWAYBAR

FRONT	REAR

TIME

NOTES:

_____

_____

_____

_____

RUN #3

	DRIVER SIDE	PASSENGER SIDE
FRONT TIRE PRESSURE		
REAR TIRE PRESSURE		
FRONT SHOCK		
REAR SHOCK		

SWAYBAR

FRONT	REAR

TIME

NOTES:

_____

_____

_____

_____

RUN #4

	DRIVER SIDE	PASSENGER SIDE
FRONT TIRE PRESSURE		
REAR TIRE PRESSURE		
FRONT SHOCK		
REAR SHOCK		

SWAYBAR

FRONT	REAR

TIME

NOTES:

_____

_____

_____

_____

RUN #5

	DRIVER SIDE	PASSENGER SIDE
FRONT TIRE PRESSURE		
REAR TIRE PRESSURE		
FRONT SHOCK		
REAR SHOCK		

SWAYBAR

FRONT	REAR

TIME

NOTES:

_____

_____

_____

_____

_____

RUN #6

	DRIVER SIDE	PASSENGER SIDE
FRONT TIRE PRESSURE		
REAR TIRE PRESSURE		
FRONT SHOCK		
REAR SHOCK		

SWAYBAR

FRONT	REAR

TIME

NOTES:

_____

_____

_____

_____

EVENT #23

EVENT NAME:	DATE:
LOCATION:	WEATHER:
VEHICLE MAKE:	VEHICLE MODEL:
TIRES:	FTD:
PAX RANKING:	CLASS RANK:

COURSE SKETCH:

RUN #1

	DRIVER SIDE	PASSENGER SIDE
FRONT TIRE PRESSURE		
REAR TIRE PRESSURE		
FRONT SHOCK		
REAR SHOCK		

SWAYBAR

FRONT	REAR

TIME

NOTES:

_____

_____

_____

_____

RUN #2

	DRIVER SIDE	PASSENGER SIDE
FRONT TIRE PRESSURE		
REAR TIRE PRESSURE		
FRONT SHOCK		
REAR SHOCK		

SWAYBAR

FRONT	REAR

TIME

NOTES:

_____

_____

_____

_____

RUN #3

	DRIVER SIDE	PASSENGER SIDE
FRONT TIRE PRESSURE		
REAR TIRE PRESSURE		
FRONT SHOCK		
REAR SHOCK		

SWAYBAR

FRONT	REAR

TIME

NOTES: _____

_____

_____

_____

RUN #4

	DRIVER SIDE	PASSENGER SIDE
FRONT TIRE PRESSURE		
REAR TIRE PRESSURE		
FRONT SHOCK		
REAR SHOCK		

SWAYBAR

FRONT	REAR

TIME

NOTES: _____

_____

_____

_____

RUN #5

	DRIVER SIDE	PASSENGER SIDE
FRONT TIRE PRESSURE		
REAR TIRE PRESSURE		
FRONT SHOCK		
REAR SHOCK		

SWAYBAR

FRONT	REAR

TIME

NOTES:

_____

_____

_____

_____

RUN #6

	DRIVER SIDE	PASSENGER SIDE
FRONT TIRE PRESSURE		
REAR TIRE PRESSURE		
FRONT SHOCK		
REAR SHOCK		

SWAYBAR

FRONT	REAR

TIME

NOTES:

_____

_____

_____

_____

EVENT #24

EVENT NAME:	DATE:
LOCATION:	WEATHER:
VEHICLE MAKE:	VEHICLE MODEL:
TIRES:	FTD:
PAX RANKING:	CLASS RANK:

COURSE SKETCH:

RUN #1

	DRIVER SIDE	PASSENGER SIDE
FRONT TIRE PRESSURE		
REAR TIRE PRESSURE		
FRONT SHOCK		
REAR SHOCK		

SWAYBAR	
FRONT	REAR

TIME

NOTES:

_____

_____

_____

_____

RUN #2

	DRIVER SIDE	PASSENGER SIDE
FRONT TIRE PRESSURE		
REAR TIRE PRESSURE		
FRONT SHOCK		
REAR SHOCK		

SWAYBAR	
FRONT	REAR

TIME

NOTES:

_____

_____

_____

_____

RUN #3

	DRIVER SIDE	PASSENGER SIDE
FRONT TIRE PRESSURE		
REAR TIRE PRESSURE		
FRONT SHOCK		
REAR SHOCK		

SWAYBAR

FRONT	REAR

TIME

NOTES:

_____

_____

_____

_____

RUN #4

	DRIVER SIDE	PASSENGER SIDE
FRONT TIRE PRESSURE		
REAR TIRE PRESSURE		
FRONT SHOCK		
REAR SHOCK		

SWAYBAR

FRONT	REAR

TIME

NOTES:

_____

_____

_____

_____

RUN #5

	DRIVER SIDE	PASSENGER SIDE
FRONT TIRE PRESSURE		
REAR TIRE PRESSURE		
FRONT SHOCK		
REAR SHOCK		

SWAYBAR

FRONT	REAR

TIME

NOTES:

_____

_____

_____

_____

RUN #6

	DRIVER SIDE	PASSENGER SIDE
FRONT TIRE PRESSURE		
REAR TIRE PRESSURE		
FRONT SHOCK		
REAR SHOCK		

SWAYBAR

FRONT	REAR

TIME

NOTES:

_____

_____

_____

_____

EVENT #25

EVENT NAME: | DATE:

LOCATION: | WEATHER:

VEHICLE MAKE: | VEHICLE MODEL:

TIRES: | FTD:

PAX RANKING: | CLASS RANK:

COURSE SKETCH:

RUN #1

	DRIVER SIDE	PASSENGER SIDE
FRONT TIRE PRESSURE		
REAR TIRE PRESSURE		
FRONT SHOCK		
REAR SHOCK		

SWAYBAR

FRONT	REAR

TIME

NOTES:

_____

_____

_____

_____

_____

RUN #2

	DRIVER SIDE	PASSENGER SIDE
FRONT TIRE PRESSURE		
REAR TIRE PRESSURE		
FRONT SHOCK		
REAR SHOCK		

SWAYBAR

FRONT	REAR

TIME

NOTES:

_____

_____

_____

_____

RUN #3

	DRIVER SIDE	PASSENGER SIDE
FRONT TIRE PRESSURE		
REAR TIRE PRESSURE		
FRONT SHOCK		
REAR SHOCK		

SWAYBAR	
FRONT	REAR

TIME

NOTES:

_____

_____

_____

_____

RUN #4

	DRIVER SIDE	PASSENGER SIDE
FRONT TIRE PRESSURE		
REAR TIRE PRESSURE		
FRONT SHOCK		
REAR SHOCK		

SWAYBAR	
FRONT	REAR

TIME

NOTES:

_____

_____

_____

_____

RUN #5

	DRIVER SIDE	PASSENGER SIDE
FRONT TIRE PRESSURE		
REAR TIRE PRESSURE		
FRONT SHOCK		
REAR SHOCK		

SWAYBAR

FRONT	REAR

TIME

NOTES:

_____

_____

_____

_____

_____

RUN #6

	DRIVER SIDE	PASSENGER SIDE
FRONT TIRE PRESSURE		
REAR TIRE PRESSURE		
FRONT SHOCK		
REAR SHOCK		

SWAYBAR

FRONT	REAR

TIME

NOTES:

_____

_____

_____

_____

NOTES

NOTES

NOTES

www.ingramcontent.com/pod-product-compliance
Lightning Source LLC
LaVergne TN
LVHW061219060426
835508LV00014B/1365